SUN AND WAVES

TO NEW BEGINNINGS

JAHANVI SINGH

Made with ♥ on the Notion Press Platform
www.notionpress.com

Dear 10 year old me

I'm proud of you.

Contents

Preface

Dear reader,

This book is a beaded necklace of emotions because that's who I am. This is unfiltered me and it's only fair to you all that you see the real me. It's complex with mistakes and it can be a lot to handle at once. The first phase is where I felt sunlight on my face, the second is me breathing fresh air towards the third phase I was broken, sad and gloomy so that's what I wanted to read and therefore I ended up writing it myself. The last phase is healing, feeling light and lively. I'm sure it's a journey you would want to be a part of.

I hope reading this book makes you feel free the way writing it did for me.

Love,

Jahanvi.

Author's Note

They asked me why the book?

To sound good I'll say it's for the world to see what waking, walking, falling, flying is from the eyes of a 20 year old but lets be real. This book is home to me, I've been writing poems ever since I was in 8th grade but I've never been confident enough to present it to the world but that's not how I feel now.

I always thought no one would like to hear me but guess I was wrong, I was heard by millions on my bookstagram @life.inside.books.

Sun and waves is the definition of confidence to me that I never had. Sun has always been motivation to me, that how it sets every evening but rises every morning with new beginning and I believe it's my beginning.

Waves feel like home to me ever since I was a child, I've found comfort in water. Waves remind me to always move forward, when still they are the calmest but when they roar nothing is more powerful.

That's home to me.

To every positive comment thank you for staying, for every negative one thank you for giving me the reason to write Sun and Waves.

This book is nothing but love, and love is all I have to give.

I hope you find your lost pieces while reading my heart.

This book is my baby, my home, my hope and now it's yours, please take care of it.

WAKING

Take one step at a time,

Some days waking up is the hardest decision.

So, it took just one glance,
For my heart to jump out of ribs,
One glance to stop breathing
One glance to lose my wits.
Was it beginning of new falling?
Was it waking of new desires?
-first crush

From everything I can afford,
I choose to gift you what I need the most.
In the darkest times I'll share my light,
On rough nights I'll be your shoulder to cry,
I'll gift you understanding when you feel alone,
I'll gift you love when you need it the most.
From someone who has everything
I crave for something.
-validation

The river in me,
Found the sea in you.

I'm simple to love,
everything I love is me
and is enough for me,
sun makes me smile,
waves make me laugh,
clouds get me high,
stars always make me surprise,
I'm easy to love
Since flowers are my dopamine'
Rain is my healer,
Snow calms me,
And soil feels like home
I'm simple to love.

And it was the innocent first touch
Threading of fingers together
Coy smiles,
Shy eyes.
~blooming love of two teenagers

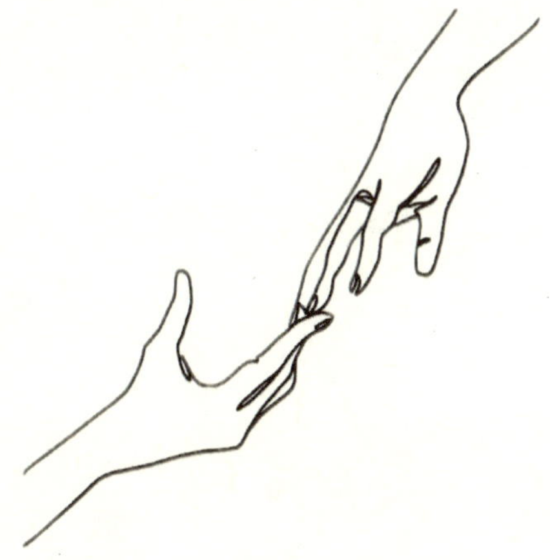

No, it wasn't the sight of you
Falling in love happened,
After knowing you.

Knowing my capability
Was enough to fight
~confidence

And you are always going to be my first,
The first touch,
The first love,
The first kiss,
The first grief,
The first loss.

And when the clouds turn grey
I run for you,
To hold me still while I cry to sleep.

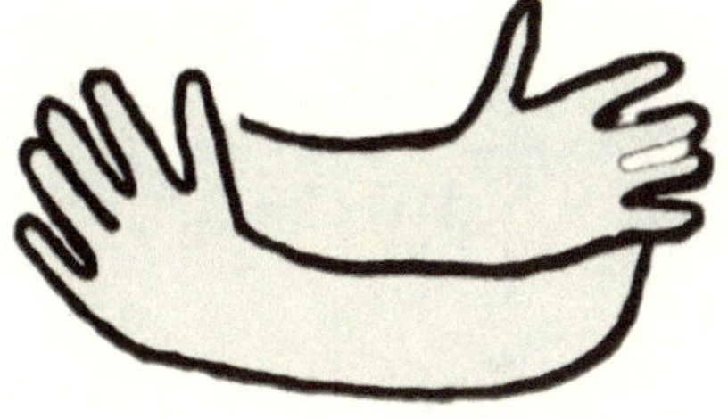

You are not my first love,
But I've every intention of making you
My last.

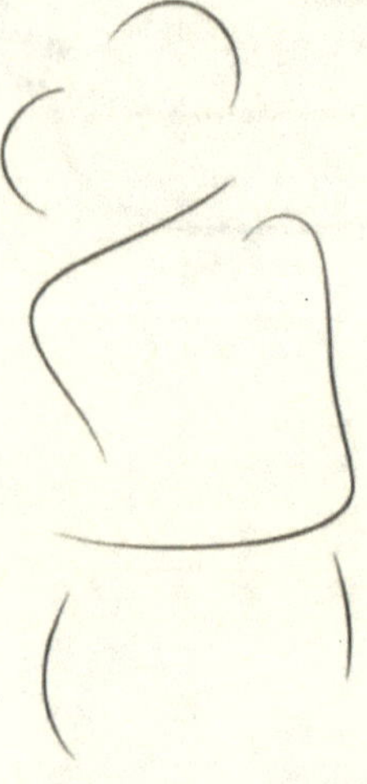

Your love is the sweetest honey that I ever tasted.

For what it's worth

I'll choose you in every life.

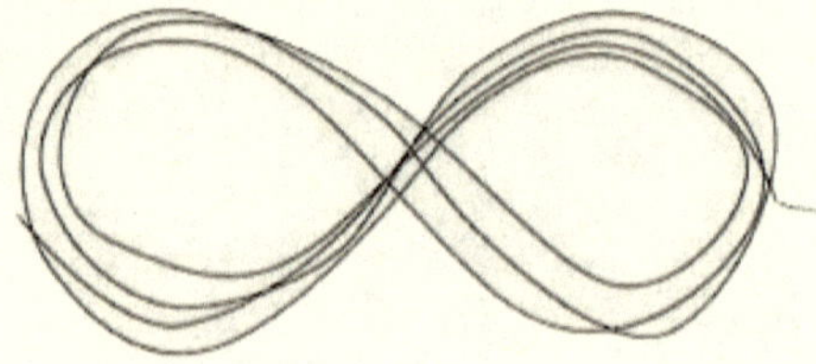

I'm going to make you a promise
Even if it scares you,
I'm staying for a long time.

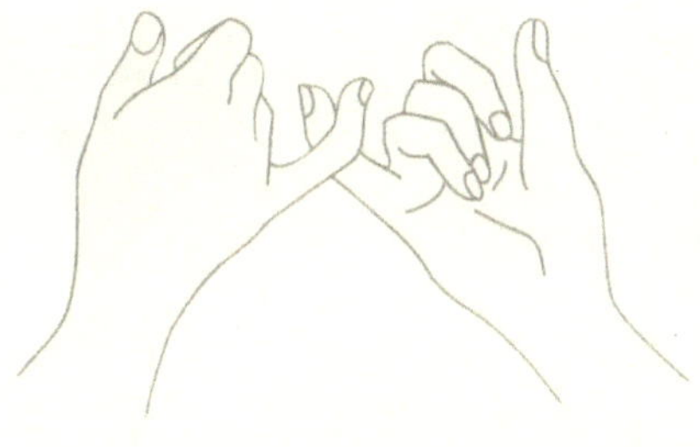

And today I woke up,
With brightest smile,
Because you were on my side.

The thing about young love is
The sincerity of heart,
The curiosity in eyes,
The trust in love,
And to dive head first in the deepest sea.

Meeting you was like finding the lost piece of my puzzle

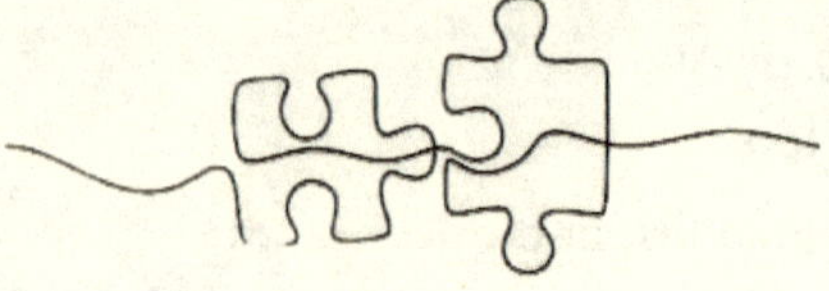

You will meet those who set your heart on fire,
You will meet those who press it cold,
And you would meet them too who set it free,
For it's them you need to keep.

Born unknown,
I thrive to grow,
Carrying thorns,
Still looking like rose
-alone

I'm a lover,
I love deep,
I love like music,
That you could only feel,
And then I met you
And you brought the lyrics.
~song of love

And I fell for you in the lost trees of autumn
But winters are lonely
So, when we start again remind me to dive in around spring
~summer love

And I believe souls exist in pairs
And life is a game to find the other player.

To the mountains where the sun rise,
To the ocean where it sets
And everything in between,
There's where hope lies,
Spreading its wings.
-hope

I was the moth blinded by your light,
Desperate for your touch,
Needy for your feel,
I was wax in your desire
Melting every second.
You ignited something that didn't existed prior.
-young love

I'll tell you what pretty is
My hair is in knots,
And my smile is crooked,
I'm not the ideal shape,
I'm tall and rigid,
Tanned and yet pale,
But you know what's pretty?
Pretty are those spots on my nose,
Pretty are the wild locks that you cannot hold,
Pretty is the smile of the crooked teeth,
Pretty is the height that wears stilettos
Pretty is the heart that sings with joy
Pretty is me for feeling like home.

I woke up today and chose to speak

-taking stand

And I never want to question you
Your affection,
Your love,
Your care,
you brought home to me.

And I didn't knew that just hearing someone's name can start a hurricane in my empty stomach.

They say don't fall for poets,
They just dress stress beautifully,
It's pretty lies wrapped in bubbles,
They say we are empty soul,
Broken hearts,
They say we are messy
And too complex to love.
But I beg your pardon
Please fall for me
Because all I've is love to give,
Under the mess and those pretty stress
Between those lines and
Lingering thoughts
Is a heart of child
Longing for love.

To be loved by you,
To be touched by you,
To be understood by you,
to be held by you,
-it was so easy to fall for you

You are perfect
Just perfect.
-you are home.

I've a habit of writing my heart on pages,
I write about love,
Like I know all it's way,
I write love letters to my every crush,
I write sonnets about those
Whom I never talked once.
But for them to fall,
Why is it always so hard?
Why they wait till the night is dark?
It took a lot for me to understand,
I can write about love
To myself.

You were my home,
Before I knew what it was,
Your embrace was the warmest blanket I ever wore
Thank you for giving me the sky,
For it's your wings I fly with.
-your loving daughter

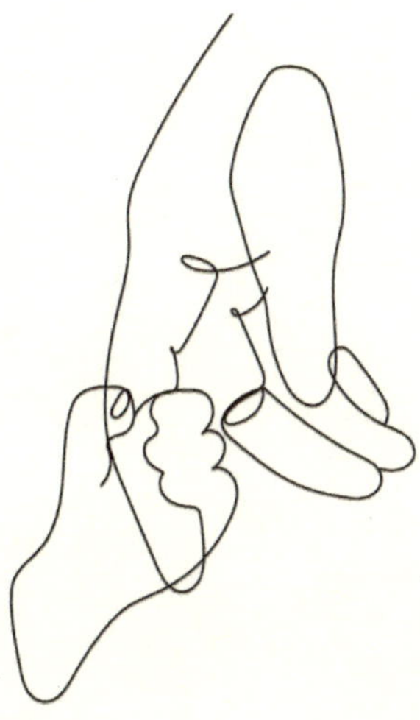

WALKING

Don't lose hope,

Keep walking

What's meant

For you

Will

Find

It's

Way

To you.

Waking next to you
Is the dream I never thought would be true.

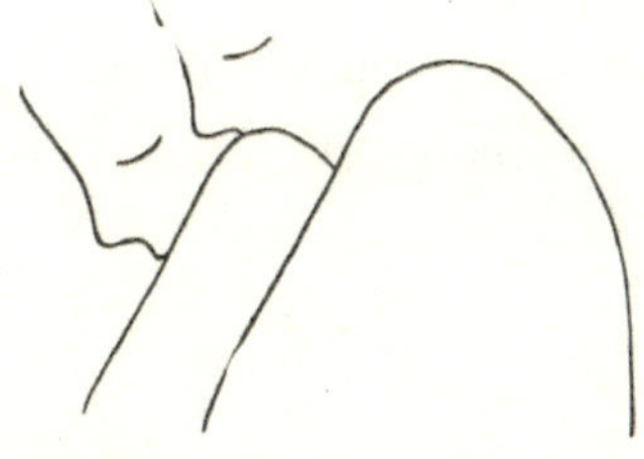

When I write about you,
I feel sorry
For the injustice I'm doing
For how kind you are
For how caring you sound
For how much love you have to give
And how beautiful your soul is bound.
These letters can never form what I see in you.
-beauty of true soul

Dear Disney,
I'm still searching for THE frog
but I escaped the tower
the glass slipper fits perfectly but
the chariot hasn't arrived yet
I had the apple,
And I'm fine.
my window is open for petter pan,
every night.
So, Flynn is my go-to type,
But charming wouldn't hurt at sight,
Now I'm sucker for library so beast may do
And if he's kind like Winnie the pooh,
Dear Disney do some bibbidi Bobbidi boo
Because this girl is delusional like anything.

"Who is writing for them?" was my question
Who? they asked
"The unpaid therapist" was my reply.
~thank you, best friend.

The idea of loving unconditionally
Leaves me in doubt.
Is it possible to not want anything
When you garden them with blood in drought.
-guess I will wait till I'm a mother.

To fall in love is beautiful
How he chose to see my eyes
Before
My lips,
My hips,
The curves and dips.
~seeing the real me

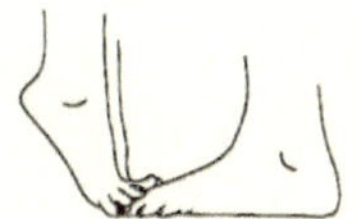

On a walk with him
He confessed
"I'm not easy to love nor easy to impress"
To my surprise it works best
I don't want easy I want complex.
-figuring each other out

It is easy to confess when moon takes over,
Giggling over little secrets,
Falling a bit more in love,
Sneaking out barefoot on grass with dew
To watch stars
To catch breaths
To feel teenage all over again.
-I feel alive with you *a little more*

When I say you are my light
I don't mean the moon
I mean the sun in February
Quietly sneaking in the winter winds.
The one that gives comfort,
The one that feels right,
I don't mean the moon
Which is someday full someday half.
I mean something which is comforting
In the chilly winter sky.
You are my sunshine.

Dear little one,
don't let them take your light
when you are meant to shine.
Keep that heart of yours always pure
Because that's what they envy most.
Use your love as a weapon
For the days that are gloomy and
Nights chilly
Love is going to give you shelter.

It's the summer 10 years ago,
I'm 10 running for pool
The biggest tension I've to bear is that
How cold water feels under my toe.
-to be a kid again.

To act asleep when you are wild awake,
For your dad to carry you to the fort of blankets,
To snuggle cozily feeling safe in the hands of the strongest man.
-I want to be 5 again.

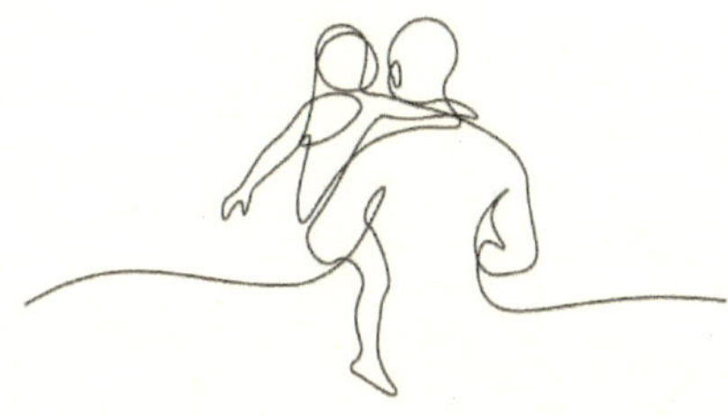

To breathe until my lungs hurt,
To laugh till my stomach aches,
To fill my eyes with tears of joy,
And to run chasing the dawn and dusk.
To cry out of fun,
To love in sorrow,
To heal in suffering,
And to grow in drought,
Is the privilege I deserve.

When we grow old, I want to have
Laugh lines and wrinkles.
When I can't stand, I want your hands in mine.
When my eyes give up on me
You would tell me
"I'm your guide".
And when the kids look at us
They'll say
"I want to be them when I age"
I want that love
-A letter from your future wife.

And I choose to sulk with you in rain
Than to have picnic with them in sun.

And if you think past was cruel,
And if think future is unfair,
~ you are wrong because you are in present.

It wasn't the face I fell for,
It was the IDEA of love.

And her body was the museum,
I prayed to be an art in.

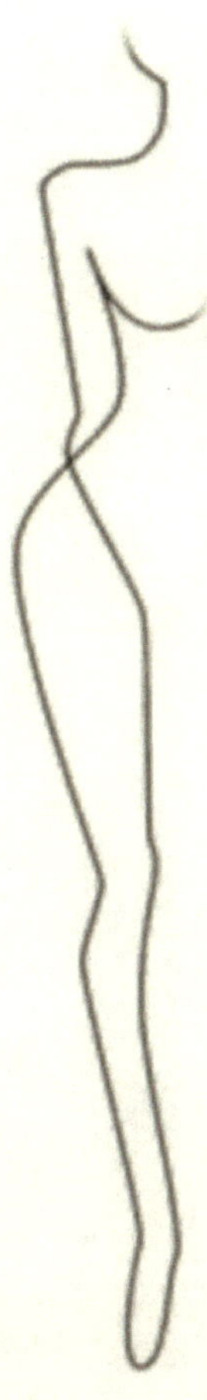

And before I knew, love knocked me out of my breath
Brought me to my knees,
And became the best thing that ever happened to me.

You deserve flowers every now and then,
You deserve to feel free,
You deserve to get handwritten notes,
You deserve kisses with lipstick stain.
If only you let me
I'll show you every day.

The thing is I will choose you in every lifetime,
That's how I love
Deeply.
Desperately.
Obsessively.
Possessively.
Strongly.

I knew it the day we met.
He smelled like the books on the oldest shelf,
Eyes of whiskey deep and doused,
Smile that freaked me out.
I wanted to read,
Read every chapter of him.
The ink was old
But stained with gold.
He had stories,
I was all ears for.
And till date
I search for him,
In every book I read.
~where are you now?

forever
and
always

If we ever meet again I'll tell you how I feel
about you,
I'll tell you everything,
how your lips taste like honey,
How your skin feels like butter,
How your eyes are the deepest ocean I have ever seen,
How your arms fit me like gloves,
How you smell like home.
When we meet again
I'll tell you everything.

Show me how broken you are,
I'll show you my shattered self,
Together we will make one,
Two bodies one soul.

I love you,

And I'll never have the answer to why.

As if for every reason I give there are thousands more to be discovered.

I love you

For one reason I know for sure.

Your love brought my soul back to life.

After having a sip of you,
I would prefer you over coffee.

You are the most beautiful person I've met
And that is an understatement.

I have a *heart,*
Fragile to touch,
I *care* too much.
I think to *overthink,*
And then *apologise,*
I *worry* a lot,
And *cry* for them,
When I know
All they do is
They can't *care* less.
I feel *trapped,*
I feel the *guilt,*
All this because
I know I won't receive
The way I *give.*

~anxiety

FALLING

Before you fly

You are meant to have a fall.

Think I'll always be drawn to you a little,
There is always going to be a string tying you to me,
I see flowers and I see your smile,
I see the sun and I'm instantly reminded how blind I'm without your light.
Because when it rains few drops escape my eyes,
And I guess that's how it's supposed to be
Because how else one can forget someone you loved so deeply.
So, there's a knot holding me to you,
I read pages and all I see are words,
I smile at mirror and there is a stranger starring back.
I feel lonely in crowd
I feel drawn to you
Because how else are you going to explain
What it feels to be unfinished.

And my mind keeps running to the dark corners of brain,
Bringing back reasons of voice why I'm not capable to stay.
Was I born with such doubts?
Or did I evolved to love them?
The stranger in my head
Put daggers deep to push me into stress
Did I come out of the womb
Questioning every name?
-depression

Am I enough?
Beautiful enough?
Brave enough?
Fun enough?
Ever enough?
-DOUBTS

I change seven times a day.
Reflections are questioning
How much do I age?
Do I deserve you,
Am I your trophy girl?
Perfect for society,
But never enough to love.

Put me through hell,
Punch me in guts,
Tell me I'm not worthy enough.
Tell me I'm broken to love.
Drag me to secret corners,
Bruise every inch of me,
Just free those screams out of me
Because I want something again to feel.
-numb.

I've known I deserve better,
I've known my worth
How foolish was I
To even lose a breath over you,
When you not cared enough to look once.
How foolish of me to low my guards,
When you built wall of thorns.
I craved
Craved
One touch
when she was getting them all.
How foolish of me,
Not to fight.
How foolish of me to fall.

I still find you in,
Rain drops,
Sad songs,
Long walks,
Tea stalls,
Monday blues,
And everything between those untied loose loops.

It wasn't from the back
The knife came right in face,
Executed so well,
That I question till date.
Was he right?
I was wrong?
Wasn't I?
Cold and unbothered,
I was walking corpse.
Imprisoned in pain,
his pain.
He had mask under masks.
And a face charming like hell.
His hands were clean
But the crime was done,
He's walking free
Without any remorse,
When I'm left undone.

So how does it feel to have everything under control?
I'm a mess.
When sad
I'm a fountain of tears.
When happy
I glow.
Anger doesn't suit me well
I burn,
But it's never on face.
I love extensively
Emotions always overflow.
Heartbreaks shatter me
And I always search my soul.
Is it good be so emotional?
Is it good to feel so much?
Is it ok to care for everyone?
And get attached to every soul?

Some people don't realize how bitter they are
Unless you start carrying a mirror for there every word.

I rented them a room in my heart,
But they all lost the keys.

And they asked
"Why are you kind to everyone?"
It took everything in me not to cry
I whispered
"Because some made me realize how deep words can cut."

When you reach the stars,
Just remember you started from dust.

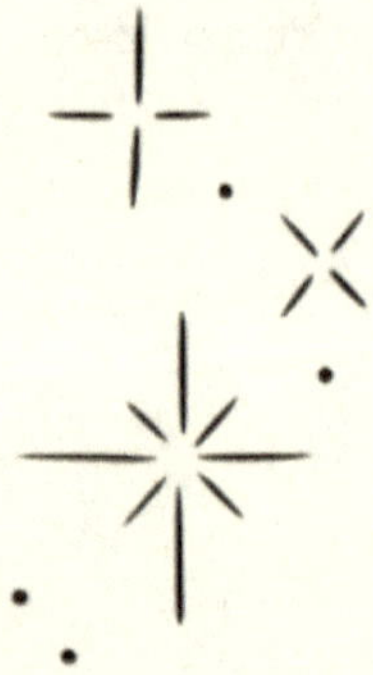

Have you ever felt uncomfortable,
In what you called your COMFORT ZONE.

She looks like cloud,
That Everyone can easily fall into.
The thing is she is like clouds
You can never hold her.

Now I know why they don't fall for me.
It's me who's to blame
Because I don't let you ever see the real me.
~insecure.

Mornings are the hardest these days,
You don't wake me to wish a beautiful day.

I trusted them to carry knives,
I just forgot to wear the shield.

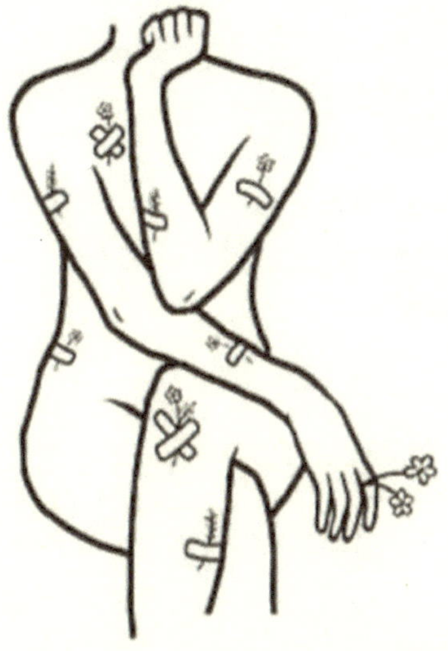

To that little girl,
I'm sorry I never made you feel loved.
You need to heal,
You need to feel,
The traps are there,
But you are brave to escape,
I'm sorry they ignored,
I'm sorry I never told
"You are worthy"

The good thing is you weren't my soulmate.
The bad thing is I believed you were.

The thing about love is
It leaves your lips stained.

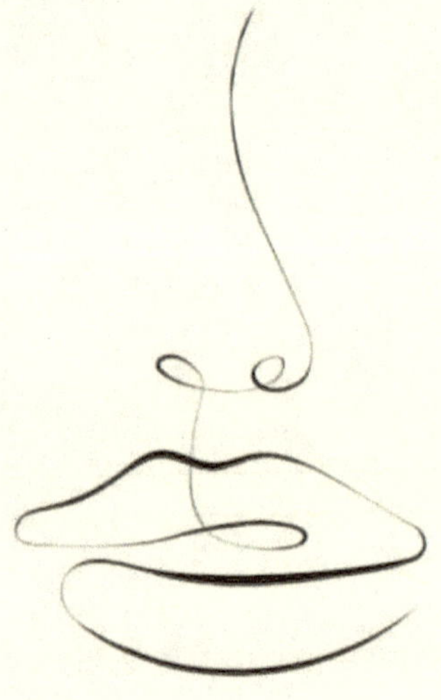

I hate how I can still smell you in my shirt.

Its suffocating,
But that's how they choke you,
They kill the child in you first,
Then spill fake responsibilities,
Next comes the pressure of success,
They poison your passion,
And then burry your dreams.
Lastly, they want you to smile
For society to please.
-pressure of society.

And he loved me like moon,
Some days full,
Bright and blinding.
Some days half,
Making me unsure.
Somedays quarter,
Doubting.
Somedays not at all.

I don't want you to fight my battles,
Just support me in them.

So that's what I learned,
Obsession is not love,
Nor is insecurity,
Love isn't ignorance,
Love isn't possession.
Its freedom.

To be loved,
Self love is important.

He said I'm pretty,
I gushed.
Then he said the same thing
To the next passing girl.
I guess after all
I wasn't that special.

Sometimes apologies never come,
You should just move on.

It was time for me to leave,
not because I loved you less,
but Because staying made me hate myself more.

Sometimes when its dark in night
Your memories make their way to my eyes,
Sneaking through that little creak
it flows down my cheek,
leaving trails like you did.

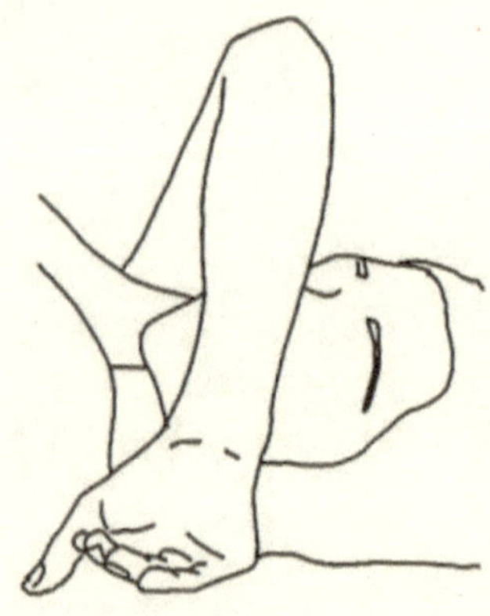

I wish I could skip this part,
The longing,
The breaking,
The tearing,
All that we had in past.

It took me long to realise,
If I mattered,
I wouldn't have to keep asking,
If I do.

I was a field of roses
But you
Were afraid of thorns.

By now I should have been used to people leave
Still, I stand here
Surprised
Because
I believed when you said
“I’ll stay for a long time.”

They never warned me
But they should.
Breakup with friends should come with
DISCLAIMERS.
I can't emphasise enough,
It hits like tsunami,
It stings, it burns.
It's the worst.
~the hushed heartache.

The worst part of all this is
We loved so much
That it didn't worked at all.

So dad do you remember when was the last time I hugged you?
Was it when you came home after loads of work? Was it when I scrapped my knee? or was it, when I came yelling to show that toy?
When was the last time you hugged me in those arms?
Was it when I failed an exam? Was it when I aced one? Was it when I left home? Was it when I lost hope?
- I miss those arms of yours.

FLYING

It's liberating to even stand up again after a fall

imagine how flying would feel like.

I didn't stop,
Believe me I wanted to.
I didn't stop
Because
I deserved a chance.
I kept going,
Because
I wanted not to give up
On myself .
I wanted someone to
Trust me.

Dear little one,
Before you make plans
About spending lifetime with them,
Make sure you can
Spend eternity with yourself first.

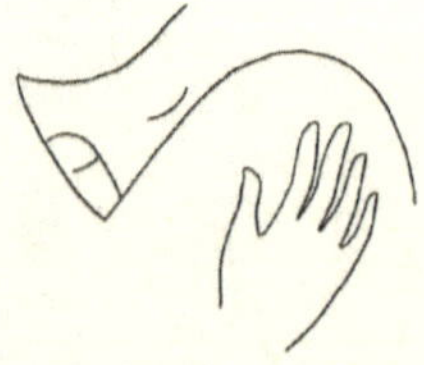

So, they said I have phases,
The good thing is
So does the moon.
It's good to have somethings hidden than to open up all.

Even after this all
I'll tell the little me to love with her whole heart,
The future me to push it even hard.
After all love is what they fear.

In spite it all
Here you are living
You did a great job.

I remember being her,
Lowering her guards
Loving the wrong ones,
To give them all
To receive not even half.
I chose to trust,
I chose to love,
Because
I thought my love was
Enough.

Just like the moon
This phase will also pass
Today you are low,
And some days even half
But
At the end
You are always full.

It's not just ok to be emotional,
It's beautiful to be emotional,
It's beautiful to have sides,
It's beautiful to love without conditions,
It's beautiful to feel.
-don't consider it weak it's your strength.

Look

Look how far you have come,

Look how much you have grown,

Look how much you have learned.

Look how beautifully you lived,

Look how much you travelled,

Look how much you fought.

Look how passionately you are loved,

Look how much you give,

Look how much you deserve.

- the road might be a rough one but it's not over yet.

Hey little one,
I'm proud of what you have become
For the things no one sees.
How you take stand when speaking is pain,
I'm proud of how confident you are,
For how you guard yourself,
For how you love,
And how you care.
I'm proud
That you don't shy away from emotions,
And that you let the tears flow.
I'm proud of how much you have grown,
~to my 10 year old self

It's hurting today,
But it will heal.
the wound is deep,
But the scars will roar
Bravery.

You will hurt
You will hurt
A lot.
The pain will sting
And burn like flames.
But after the sun sets
You will rise again.

You know what let's do this again,
It won't be our first date.
Take me on a fourth one
Where I know you just enough,
A handsome face,
With Droopy smile.
Let's have candy floss,
Thread our hands together,
And have a Walk in the park after sun sets.
Tell me about your favourite show,
Show me how you giggle,
And how you love,
And when the evening ends
Kiss me like fireworks.
Let's communicate for once.

I didn't knew human heart was so strong,
Breaking, shattering
Over and over again
Still managing to beat.

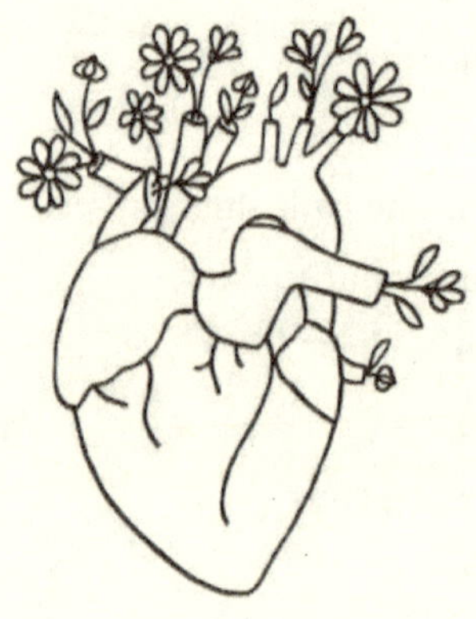

Sometimes it's hard to accept,
But the battles that give you the deepest cuts
Are ones you never fought.
~surrender

You know reading books is easy,
If they are being toxic
You can always close the chapters and take a break.

You know why I love sunsets?
It's because it reminds me
That I'll always have tomorrow.
The sky will burn for me again,
The birds will wait for me to wake them,
If today was hard,
There is always a tomorrow.

I know you are afraid of love,
They always leave
Don't they?
So, this time lets fall for constants,
The sunrays,
Fall for new today.
The pretty books,
And hot tea in winter mornings.
Until someone is brave enough to break those walls.

Hey little one,
It's a reminder
Life is unpredictable
So go on that trip,
Wear that little dress,
Dye your hair,
Be extra
Cry out of laughing hard and
Cry until you laugh,
Live.

Loosing you reminded me,
To love myself.
-becoming

Hey,
I hope when they call you pretty next time,
They mean,
That you are radiant like sunrays,
They mean it when they say you sparkle,
And your light is blinding.
I hope they mean it in a way that you being clumsy
Is you being kid at heart.
I hope the next time they call you pretty is because
You are enough to light a room,
You make tables turn
With confidence and not just looks.
I hope they realise.

After all they did
I'm on my side,
Its good have a company.

I know healing can be hard,
To heal,
you need to begin from the start.
From the first page,
First chapter,
First word.
It's not gonna be easy as they say
But it's what you need.

I know the things I lack,
But decide imperfection is beautiful.

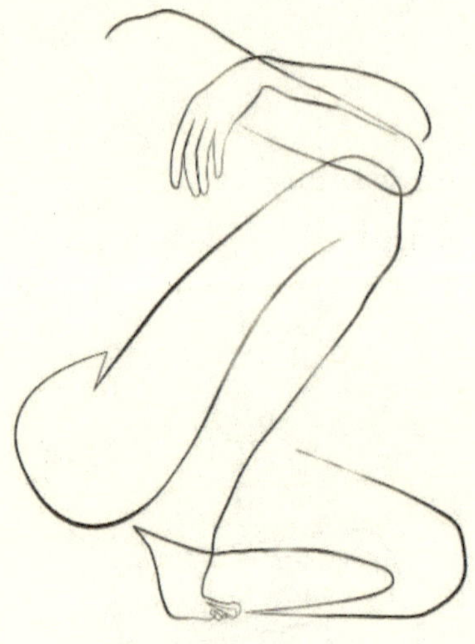

The worst thing is
You believe
That it's because of them
That you are happy.
Your joy doesn't belong to
Those Cruel palms of betrayal.
t's you
Your goals that set you free,
You are happy
For
What you have achieved.
Your joy is your possession
Its not them who makes you happy.
-Happiness

Stop convincing

That you are happy.

Your heart and mind both chose different wars.

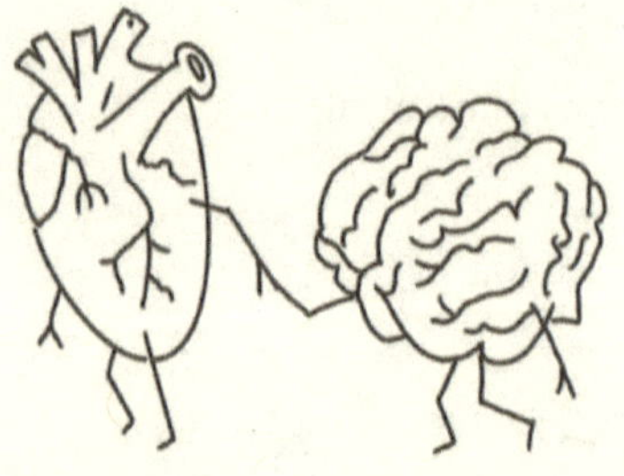

Little one,
Breathe for me
One breath at a time.
Repeat after me
"I won't apologise
For the loving soul I have,
For the pure heart that survived,
For the body that has seen a lot,
For the beautiful mind that trusted them all.
Because
I'm alive
I'm wanted,
I'm brave."
Little one can you promise me that?

"so, even after that all, you are a romantic at heart?"
Yes!
Because I have hope I'll fall for someone once more,
I'm not *hopeless* I'm *hopeful.*
Hopeful about finding love,
Hopeful about running into the arms that feel like home,
Hopeful about seeing sunset on beaches with someone I call love.
Hopeful for someone to tuck me in a blanket,
When I pass out on couch drunk.
Hopeful is the word I use.
I'm a hopeful romantic.

Journey

It's not your fault
There is nothing wrong with you at all.
In the process,
You felt used,
You lost hope,
You trusted wrong,
What you feel is fear,
What you feel now is you
Alive.

It takes time,
It takes years for the seed to become a tree.
~blooming

Hey little one,
Your restless mind
Doesn't need to have all the answers,
So, take one step at a time. .

It's a gone shot for me to pretend,
I won't lie
I want love,
But it's my heart that needs time,
And I care for her a lot.

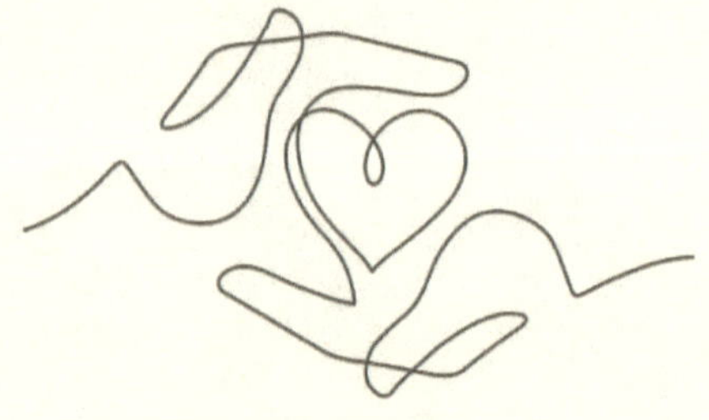

maybe not today but some day
you will realise,
it's for the best
they left,
you will
survive
without
them.

little one,
don't you dare lower your worth.
You are valuable.
Don't you dare give them your light,
When you lay in dark.
Don't you dare to make room for them
And live in dust.
For what it matters
You are loved.

Dear Reader,

You have made it to the end,

Thank you for reading my heart, diving in my soul, I feel heard. I know it was a rocky road so take a breath for me, will you?

For all it's worth you have all my attention. Thank you for sparing your time for me, I bend down to you, let me kiss those eyes and take the weight of your heavy heart.

Whether you liked it or not you gave me your time and I'm grateful, all I can give you is love. Can you please give yourself a hug from me? Wrap those arms around.

You are heard,

You are loved,

I love you.

~write yourself a love letter you deserve that.

www.ingramcontent.com/pod-product-compliance
Lightning Source LLC
LaVergne TN
LVHW091326150826
845673LV00006B/1784